I Have A New Dream

Written & Illustrated by
Davidd "DaveySoArt" Sudberry

I H A N D ™

I Have A New Dream

ISBN: 978-0-692-15206-5

Greetings Beloved!
I am honored to be here with you today.

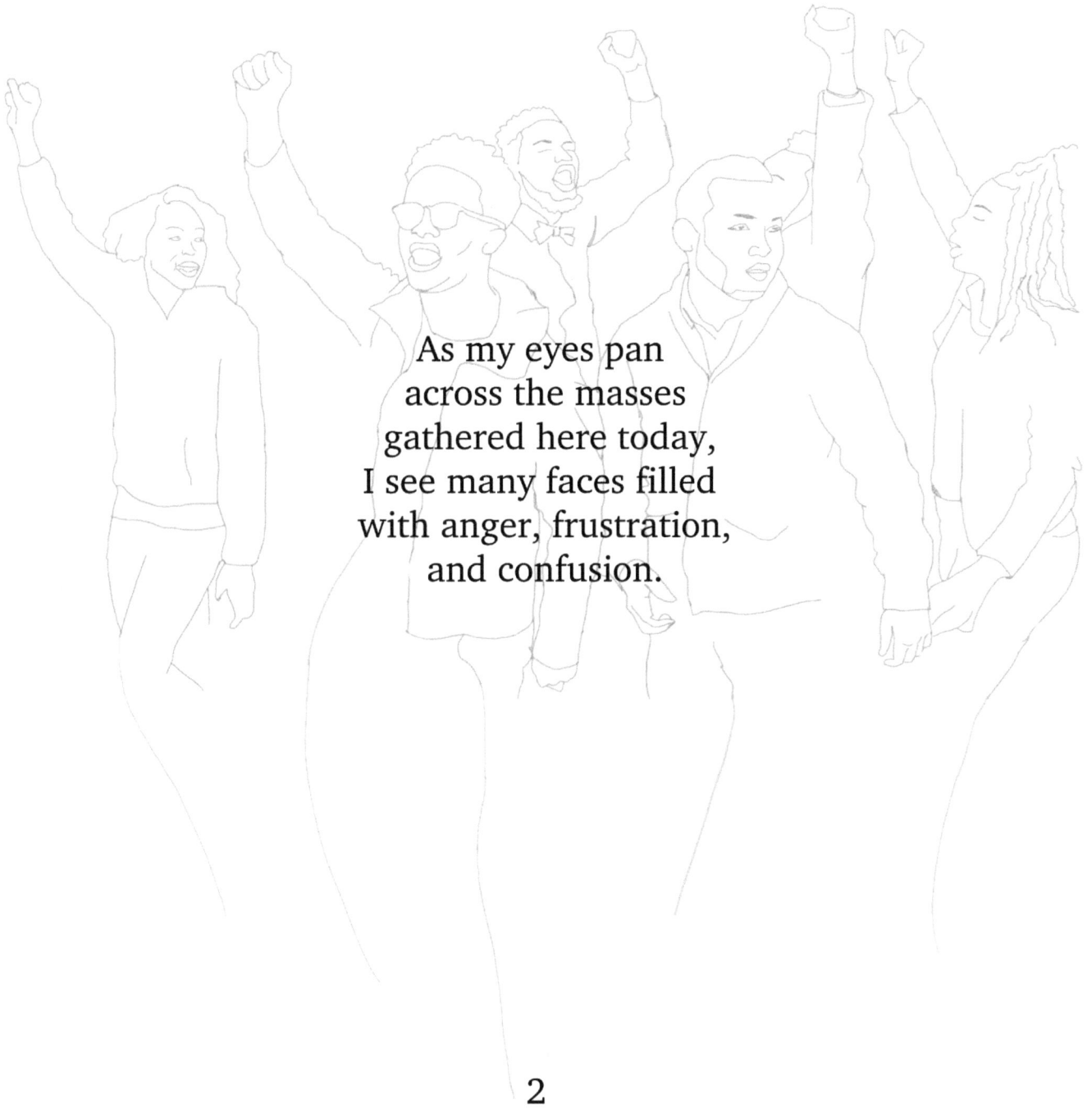

As my eyes pan
across the masses
gathered here today,
I see many faces filled
with anger, frustration,
and confusion.

1963

WE DEMAND

WE DEMAND
EQUAL
RIGHTS
NOW

WE DEMAND

2018

4

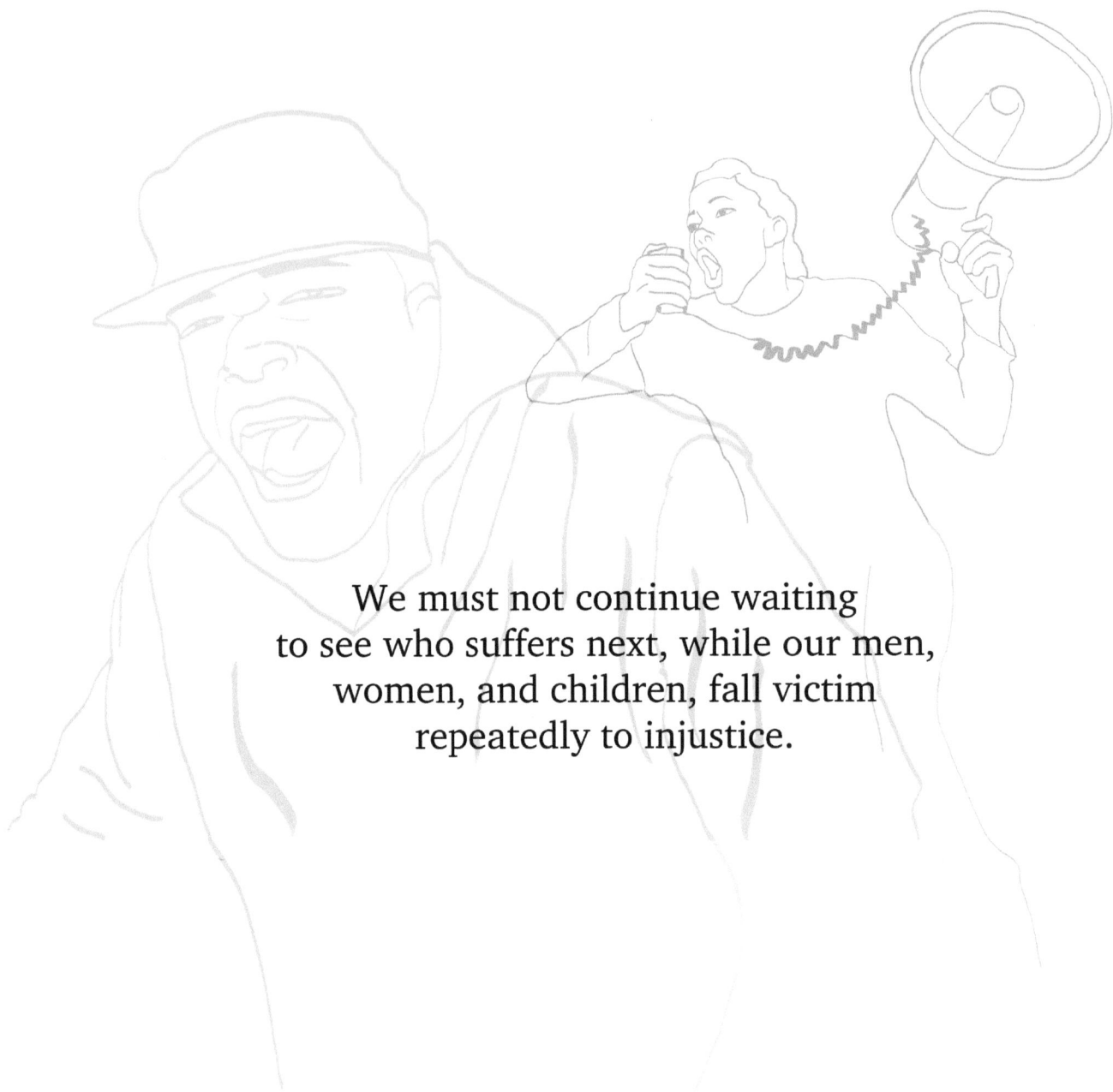

We must not continue waiting
to see who suffers next, while our men,
women, and children, fall victim
repeatedly to injustice.

Today is the day
we begin the lengthy process
of redirecting our emotions,
and energy into efforts
that will actually work.

It is a dream nourished
by the blood, sweat and tears
shed by our ancestors, as they
built this nation.

In order to make this new dream
become a reality, we must work
together with the same persistence
as they did.

Except this time beloved...

...WE BUILD FOR US!

This time we build for our children,
our grandchildren, and the future
generations to come.

We must bring together our businesses into a single location, such as a shopping plaza, or district. This is called aggregation. By doing this, we assure the money will exchange within our hands several times. This has to happen across the country wherever we are the majority of the population.

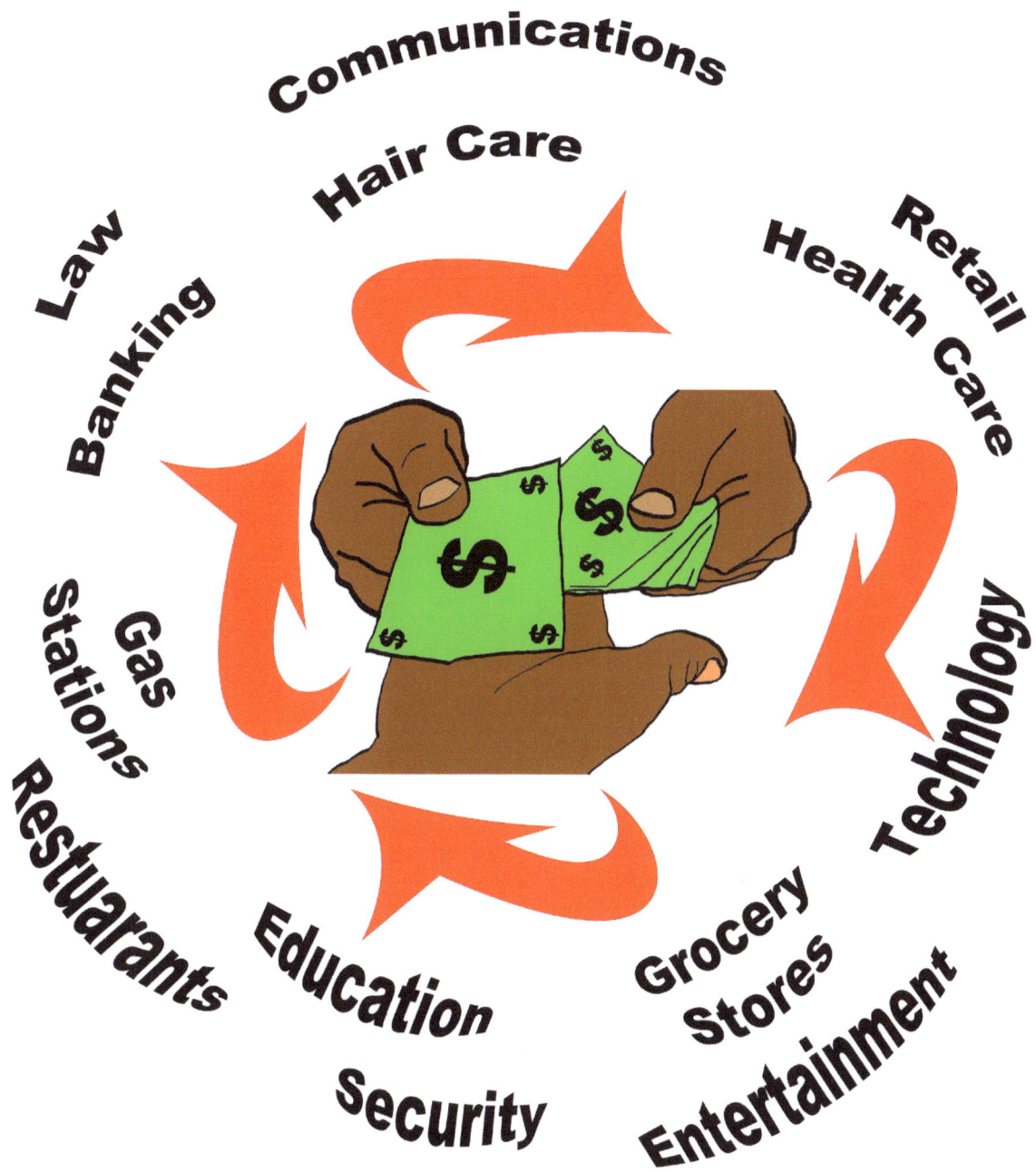

Communications

Hair Care

Law

Banking

Retail

Health Care

Gas Stations

Restuarants

Technology

Education

Grocery Stores

Security

Entertainment

With the guidance and labor
from our bravest educators,
we can redefine what education
means to us.

By tailoring the
education to fit our
economic needs, we can
produce the quality of
professionals we need to
build prosperous communities.

Many of the vacant lots around
the inner city are filled with
trash and void of purpose. This
only serves as a reminder of
our pitiful circumstance.

15

Let's purchase this land, clean it
up, and use it for inner-city farming.
These farms will serve as agricultural
training grounds from seed to harvest,
to commercial trade.

I HAVE A NEW DREAM!

One day, the mentallity of getting out of the hood to move to the suburbs will not exist amongst us. Instead, when we prosper economically, we'd reinvest in the impoverished areas that we, and many of our families grow up in. This is how you fight against gentrification and build a sense of community.

Between our banks, real estate
agents, and contractors, we
have the resources we need to
rebuild the dilapidated houses that
plague many of our neighborhoods.

19

Let us show our greatness by creating
the living conditions we desire from
the same enviroments we started in.

Unfortunately, we have been mass consumers and 0% of producers while playing in a real-life game of monopoly. Some reports estimate our spending to be about 1.2 trillion dollars annually. This is not a good thing because we're only making other groups richer while we become poorer. We need our money bouncing as many times as possible within our hands before it leaves the group.

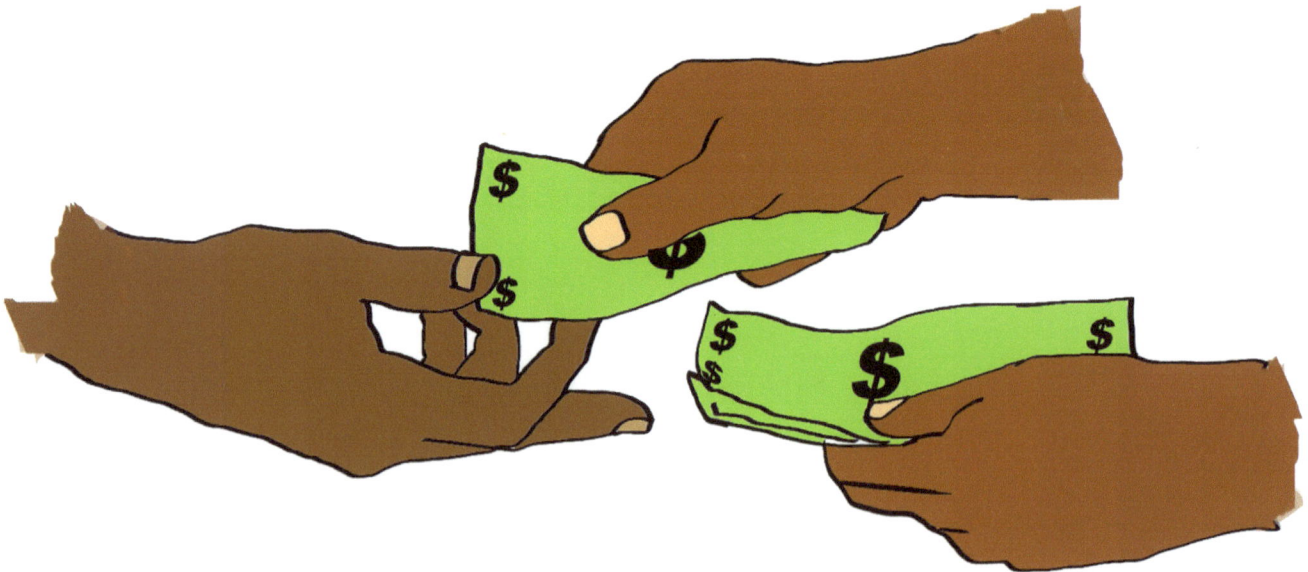

We cannot remain solely dependent on other groups for the resources we need to survive. We need more risk takers amongst us. We need entrepreneurs and investors who want to create economic opportunities for our people to prosper.

Too many of our young men never reach their potential in life, because they seek financial gain from the streets. The result is, we as a whole miss out on generations of electricians, engineers, technology innovators, scientists and such.

If those of us who are most successful would begin reinvesting into these same underserved areas, which many of us come from, we'd see dramatic changes in education and economic opportunities provided. If we don't supply the resources for our young men to succeed, nobody will.

These changes will unlock unlimited doors for our young boys, and girls alike. We have to excell much more often in fields that require math and science, as opposed to sports, and other forms of entertainment.

We have much more to offer ourselves and we have much more to give to the world. We are capable of developing cures for diseases, designing multimillion dollar facilities and so much more.

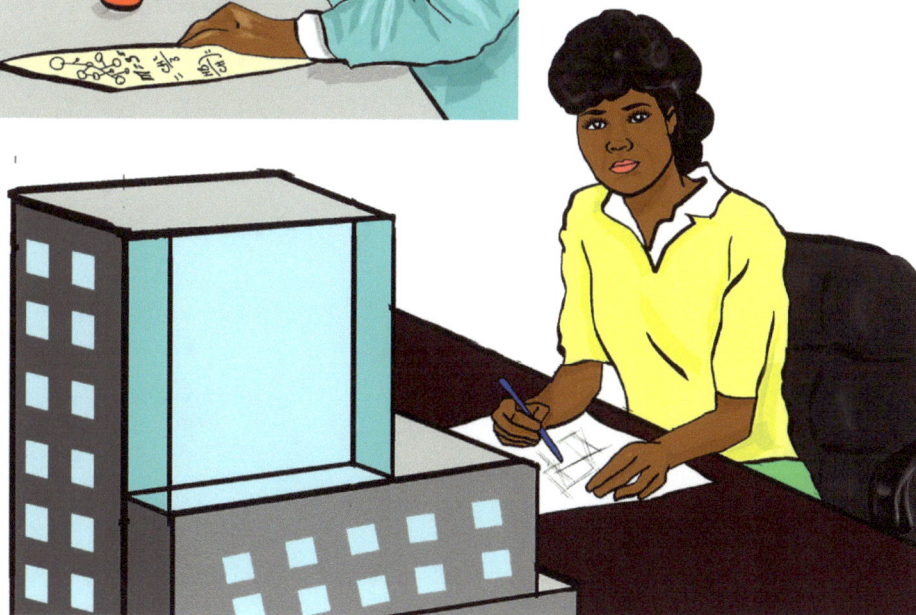

This will not be easy, but if we change
spending habits by investing in our
businesses, both as consumers and
as entrepreneurs, we can begin to
right this ship. By doing this in just half
the numbers we protest and riot with, we
could turn every ghetto, in every city
into a wealthy metropolis.

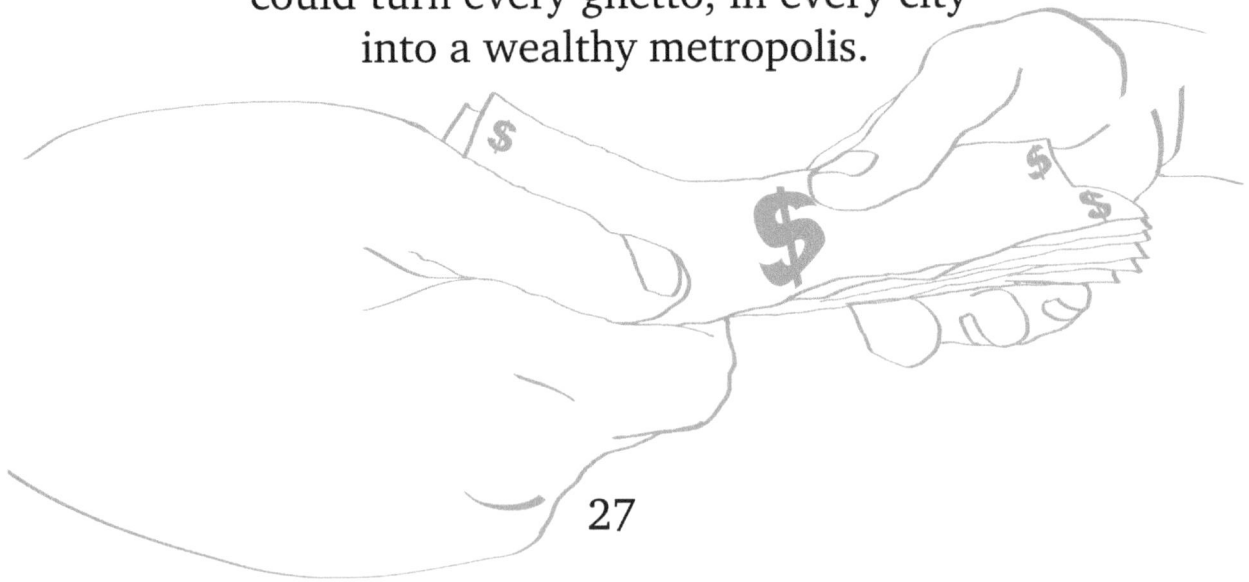

I have a new dream.

I HAVE A NEW DREAM.

I HAVE A NEW DREAM!

THE
BEGINNING

Getting Started

Make a list of every black-owned business you can think of. Be sure to include local and online companies. Do a Google search to find a black business directory today. Update your list as needed.

(List company or website)

Now that we've identified a few businesses to patron, let's keep track of our favorite companies and products. Write these down and send positive feedback to the company for encouragement. Lastly, recommend your favorite items to your family, friends, and co-workers.

(Company or Products)

Okay. You've made some purchases and spread the word to family and friends. Now let's make a list of your ride or dies. This is your tribe. These are people in your life whom you can hold accountable and they will in return hold you accountable. Start your own social network as consumers. Buy black as much as possible, trade information with one another, and share new products with yourselves as well as others.

(Contacts)

www.ingramcontent.com/pod-product-compliance
Lightning Source LLC
Chambersburg PA
CBHW042117040426
42449CB00002B/82